SELECTED POEMS OF JAMES ELROY FLECKER

WITH AN INTRODUCTION
BY
JEAN CANTLIE STEWART
MA, DIP.ED, BARRISTER-AT-LAW OF MIDDLE TEMPLE

ISBN 978-1-9993269-1-3

First published in 1999

Published by Rowan Books
Edinburgh and London

Contents

INTRODUCTION

Flecker wrote in the *Grecians*, 'To my mind a passion for beautiful things is the possession of the wise and thoughtful'. Little wonder that Keats was Flecker's favourite poet, for Keats wrote in his poetry, 'Beauty is truth and truth beauty - that is all ye know on earth and all ye need to know'. Flecker saw in everyday life, 'a beauty older than the world and greater than all its evil'. He rated the 'intellect, beauty, truth and the life of the spirit' above materialism and the pursuit of power. He hung on to this idealism, although threatened by illness and early death - which came to him aged 30 in 1915 - and although it had become, in the midst of World War I, little more than 'a meadow in a waste of sand'. His poetry is alive with colour, light, sound and music. Geraldine Hodgson in her *Life of James Elroy Flecker* said that his poems are, 'a stream of sunlight water, of transparent and many hued light'. Flecker spoke eight modern and ancient languages, and he drew on his knowledge of the Orient for ideas and word images and on the French Parnassians for examples of form and cadence. To Flecker, poetry was a combination of acute perception and intellectual and emotional activity and, in order to develop these creative gifts, the poet needed 'an enthusiasm for the world in every detail' - a world that was always 'passionately interesting' and filled with human kindness. He was not a great classical scholar, because he did not value detailed accuracy sufficiently high, but he was steeped in the scholasticism of many countries, which he evidenced in his translations, and he demanded a place in human existence for the quenching of the thirst of the human spirit as well as of that of the body. Because of his love of perfection he wrote and rewrote, mastering words and techniques in an age when many poets were experimenting with and drifting into formlessness.

James Elroy Flecker was born in November, 1884. His paternal grandfather was a schoolmaster in Constantinople, his grandmother was of Huguenot descent. His maternal grandfather was a Hebrew scholar, who contributed to the 1884 English version of the Bible. His father took Holy Orders in the Church of England and became headmaster of a London school and then of Dean Close School, Cheltenham. James inherited from him a lifelong interest in education and teaching and, in these halcyon days before Shaw's sneering remarks had undermined the confidence of the teaching profession, he saw a successful schoolmaster's life as a pinnacle of achievement, only attained with a first class honours degree. His mother had been a student at the Royal Academy of Music and she encouraged her children to play together in a family orchestra. Flecker attended Dean Close School from the age of eight and then went on to Uppingham for 5 terms, where he won an open classical scholarship to Trinity College, Oxford, which he attended as an undergraduate from 1902-6. He loved Oxford, being a great talker and friend, and became a member of the bohemian set, whose members enjoyed exotic literature. Getting a third in Mods shook his confidence, but, although this setback made him work harder at writing his own verses and studying French literature, he still did not apply himself sufficiently hard to the classics or metaphysics (the latter of which he hated) until it was too late. Nevertheless, he did not expect his third in Greats, and, after two years spent teaching, tutoring and travelling, his knowledge of modern and classical languages won him a vacancy as a student-interpreter in the Foreign Consular Service and two years' preliminary study at Caius College, Cambridge, before being posted to Constantinople in 1910, where he was appointed Vice Consul.

What sort of a man was Flecker? J.C. Squire described him as tall with blue eyes, straight hair and dark complexion, with a tinge of the East in his appearance and an expression which bore a blend of the sardonic and the gentle. As a child he was determined, observant and sensitive to the point of being nervous, with a temper which flared suddenly and an obstinacy that was difficult for adults to overcome. He adopted his parents' religious beliefs until Oxford days, when he became agnostic, returning to his religious roots later in life. From early days his parents read aloud to their children, poetry as well as prose classics. Flecker wrote poetry all his life and the poems of his boyhood show the same lilt, rhyme, alliteration and assonance as those of later life. Already, in his early work, can be seen his love of nature and the joys and griefs of human life, together with a depth of feeling and an awareness of religion, mysticism and the desire for peace, perhaps the most elusive of mankind's needs. In the words of George Herbert, the seventeenth century metaphysical poet, when God dispensed his pile of blessings, 'Peace at the bottom lay'. It is impossible when reading Flecker's poetry not to believe that he foresaw his early death, which, if it had not come from consumption, would in all probability have been brought about by the First World War, the distant rumblings of which could be heard by those in his generation who had the ears to hear. Cambridge University, which he attended from 1908 to 1910, did not recreate for Flecker the same idyllic happiness as he had experienced at Oxford - the flatness of the Fens depressed him - but he made friends and left his mark in his second year. He loved his translating work and, with his mind turning now to the study of modern Eastern languages, he might, had he lived longer, have introduced original Oriental literature into the United Kingdom in the same way as he did French forms and verse. Already in these early days he was getting good reviews for his poems and translations and his fellow students were beginning to recognise his genius.

Tragically his consumption began only months after his arrival in the East. Very hot after a ride, he dived into the Black Sea for a swim and, suffering after-effects, consulted a doctor, who found traces of the dreaded disease. He was sent back to a sanatorium in the Cotswolds, which countryside he loved with a passion that lasted all his life, growing in strength as his later exile in Switzerland continued. The nursery of his childhood days had faced south over a rose garden to woods and hills, with the Cotswolds beyond, and this scene recurs frequently in his poetry, when, sick and far from his beloved England, he dreams and dreams that he is home again. During the second three months of his sick leave he was less quiescent and more rebellious about the restrictions placed on him, so that, once out of the sanatorium, he began to enjoy life once more and work again at his writing. In Paris he was fortunate to meet Mademoiselle Helle Skiadaressi, a Greek lady to whom he became engaged and later married - an earlier unofficial engagement to another girl having come to nothing. His friend Frank Savery said that Flecker relied greatly on his wife's taste - not only did her devotion prolong his life, but her 'acute feeling for literature helped to confirm him in his lofty ideals of artistic perfection'.

While in Paris he was posted to Smyrna, but after marriage, temporarily delayed because of a relapse in health, he was posted instead to Beirut. As in Constantinople, he loved his work, proving himself 'a good business official', and yet finding time to write poetry and plays, but he found the Lebanon arid and airless, which affected his health and that of his wife. On leave in England he therefore tried to transfer to a post at home, and, when this proved unsuccessful, his parents offered him a house and allowance, which he did not accept, wishing to be independent. Returning to Beirut alone, leaving his wife to recover from a bout of fever at her parents' home in France, he suffered almost at once from a recurrence of consumption. His wife joined him immediately, and, after a spell in hospital in Beirut, Flecker went - now desperately ill - to a sanatorium in Leysin, Switzerland and thence to other sanatoriums in Montreux, Montana, Locarno and finally Davos, where he died in January, 1915.

Although Flecker drew on wider sources than the majority of his contemporaries and, in J.C. Squire's view, his illness detached him from them, nevertheless he was held by reviewers to be a typical poet of the 'Georgian nest of singing birds', whose number included Rupert Brooke, Francis Thompson, G.K.Chesterton, Walter de la Mare, A.E. Houseman, W.B.Yeats, John Masefield, W.H.Davis and Wilfred Owen. The Georgian Poets were so-called because they took poetry back into the lyrical warmth of feeling of the past. They reacted against the cynical, sophisticated worldliness of writers such as Wilde, and aimed at 'rediscovering the purpose of existence and the individual impulses of the human heart'. They thus reawakened the aims of the Romantic Movement of a century earlier, with its love of nature and the beauty and meaning of everyday life. Although experimenting with freer patterns, they wrote mostly in disciplined rhyme and metre, not shifting the rules too far away from the Classical, Elizabethan, Miltonian and Romantic models, and from the ballad metre of a simpler age. Much of their poetry had an underlying seriousness in its message. For more than two decades before the outbreak of World War I the young men of that generation saw the great clash coming between two widely different types of Western civilisation, the democratic way of life in Britain, France and other smaller Western European countries and the controlled military concept of government represented by Bismark's new Germany. For the first time in history Germany now straddled the continent, united by the award to Prussia at the Congress of Vienna in 1815 of the Rhinelands and Wesphalia, which enabled Bismark to pincer the German states into a customs and then a political union, leading to the creation of a consolidated but undemocratic modern state, with no representative organ of government given power to control the vast army or navy estimates. Even the young men of the 1930's watching Hitler's raucous outpourings, were not as aware for so long a period of the price they would have to pay in defence of freedom. Early twentieth century literature needs to be read against this sad political background, which gave the young men of this doomed generation an underlying similarity of outlook, expressed in accordance with their own genius and character.

The poetry of James Elroy Flecker and Rupert Brooke, two of the leading poets of the Georgian Movement, represents the aspirations, inspiration and composition of the age, while their lives ran parallel to each other both in background and duration. Each poet acts as a foil to the other - yet, while Brooke's poetry is available in the bookshops, Flecker's is not. J.C. Squire wrote in the Introduction to the 1916 edition of Flecker's *Collected Poems* that Rupert Brooke broke the news of his death to him over the telephone. They were almost exact contemporaries, for Brooke was born in 1887, 3 years after Flecker, and died from sunstroke while serving in the Royal Naval Division in the Mediterranean, where he was buried in Scyros in 1915, 3 months after Flecker's coffin was borne across the Channel to Cheltenham. Brooke's father was a housemaster at Rugby, which Rupert entered in 1901, writing poetry and excelling in friendships, games and books - winning a scholarship to King's College, Cambridge. Like Flecker, he initially found Cambridge 'rather wearying', but he came to love it and was a brilliant and popular scholar.

A comparison between the writing of these men gives a sense of perspective to their poetry and to that of the age in which they lived. Flecker's poetry was more learned than Brooke's, for he was a classicist as well as a romantic and his scholasticism gave his travels depth and meaning, while his knowledge of the East brought into modern poetry a new and challenging dimension of romance, colour, touch and sound, creating images of an unexplored and older Eastern civilisation. Temporarily deserting the Christian religion, Flecker imbibed the spiritual patterns and colours of the Moslem culture, giving fresh inspiration to his later work, which included his play *Hassan*, but he returned in the end to his own faith, hurt if not sickened by the cruelty of the Moslem world. It is claimed that Flecker drew for his early effects on Tennyson's resonance, but by his later twenties his poetry was creating an atmosphere all its own. Here was onomatopoeia at its best - the sound suiting the sense - and he had become master of the poetic arts - rhyme, repetition, alliteration, assonance - harnessing them all to create his unique imaginative and sensual effects. Love poems alternate with those of a poet sick at heart and in body, longing for his own country with its familiar sights and sounds. His use of personification make his trees, cliffs and flowers beckon him home with compelling force. He often wrote in ballad metre, his ear attuned to the musical lilt typical of the Auld Alliance of France and Scotland, and the love songs of Byron and Burns. Because of his poetic agility the forms he chose for expressing his deepest thoughts remained flexible, and his not infrequent break-away patterns of metre and verse flow so naturally and musically that they disguise the absence of his regular beat.

Like Flecker, Brooke experimented frequently, but, relying on his English antecedents, he liked the sophistication of the sonnet, showing how it could portray ordinary life, as well as the deepest aspirations of the human heart. Whereas Flecker's poetry often has a sadness, which is exquisitely haunting, Brooke's poetry, despite his similar preoccupation with early death, usually manifests exuberant enthusiasm, making the words race breathlessly through his letters and verses. While Flecker's poetry has little humour, Brooke's has much, switching suddenly from the serious to the ridiculous, and abounding with laughter, love, sunlight, the golden hours of day, the smells and sights of the world around him, and the sequence of the seasons and of day and night. Like Flecker, he constantly lamented death (or less frequently old age), which would end both the gladness and the tears, and he employed all the figures of speech to enhance his effects and the disciplines of rhyme and metre, not only to make the music of his verses flow, but also to formulate his thoughts and aid clarity and comprehension. Both poets recognised that 'painstaking artistry' is needed to 'fashion inspiration into clear and compact imagery and verse', without which poetry becomes unintelligible, isolated and remote. Although sometimes the reader might be tempted to think that Brooke's poetry is more superficial than Flecker's, nevertheless the same spiritual and humanist longings are there, the concept of the soul travelling through life in a quest for the Holy Grail, the emptiness and desolation in the ruins of revolution, the contrast between democracy and central control.

Always in the back of both men's minds is the thought of early death, and, for all his exuberance, Brooke is in many ways more pessimistic than Flecker, the self-styled 'lean and swarthy poet of despair', whose fears of a consumptive death are described in his poems *Envoy, No Coward's Song, Prayer, In Hospital* and *Felo-de-se.* There can be few more tragic poems in the English language than Brooke's two sonnets on *Death* and the later *Fragment* - on board ship in the War - in which he sees the young men of his generation as 'ghosts.. coloured shadows.. soon to die'. In his *Funeral for Youth*, written in 1913, Brooke predicted that Love would not be present at the funeral, for 'she had died long ago' while Innocence would be represented by her daughter Ignorance. In this prediction Brooke's attitude contrasts with Flecker's, for, although Flecker questioned 'whether the piper would still be playing after the war', nevertheless he thought that 'the love and kindness of the human heart' would endure, and this belief was shared by his fellow Georgian, Wilfred Owen, who - recommended for an MC just before he was killed in France in November, 1918 - wrote 'the poetry is in the pity'.

C. Day Lewis claimed that the whole Georgian Movement was 'rolled under by the war', with this phrase of Owen's the only surviving thought, but Owen showed how, despite suffering and carnage, 'mid tears and tribulation, love and compassion continued to shine through. 'I too saw God through mud' ... 'I have perceived much beauty', and, to those at home, 'Unless you share/With them in hell the sorrowful dark of hell.../You shall not hear their mirth/These men are worth your tears'. Although it seemed that much of the Christian purpose of the nineteenth century perished in the mud of Passchendaele, taking with it many of the hopes and joys that inspired Flecker and other Georgians, nevertheless man's resilience is miraculous. In the post-war years the surviving Georgians continued to sing, albeit, as Flecker forecast, on a more thoughtful note, and - against the odds and sometimes with children in the audience - Innocence was still a guest at the gathering. But Flecker, Brooke and Owen were dead, together with millions of young men of their generation, and meanwhile from across the Atlantic was coming the poetry of Ezra Pound and W.H Auden and T.S.Eliot, who, (despite Eliot's ladder to heaven in many of his later poems) spoke of a barren waste land filled with nihilism. While not dissimilar thoughts were being echoed in England, nevertheless it was Auden who introduced into poetry a new and hopeless bitter cynicism, with his lines of doggerel, 'The expert designing the long range gun/ To exterminate everyone under the Sun, /Would like to get out, but can only mutter/ 'What can I do? It's my bread and butter''.

Each century has its dreams and those of previous decades may seem remote to a generation reared in a transient age of materialism, but the present draws inspiration from the past and this may be the moment to reawaken an interest in Flecker's poetry and re-assess his position among the Georgians, the last of whom, John Masefield, the Poet Laureate, died just over thirty years ago. Poetry is emotion, joyful or sad, remembered in tranquility. It sings a song from a heart that feels. If, through pain, tragedy and tears, it has shut out the capacity to feel (as described in Owen's poem *Insensibility*) the lute is broken. Flecker's poetry lifted the spirits of ordinary people from the hum drum activities of their lives and united the seen and the unseen. Geraldine Hodgson says of his poem *To a Poet a Thousand Years Hence*, 'unquenchable spiritual intensity lies like light upon these pages'. The traditions of rhyme, cadence, metre, stanza and figures of speech, all these devices and disciplines have been employed since the dawn of time to conjure out of air a language 'sweeter or more solemn or sad than ordinary speech or prose'. From early times poetry and music went hand in hand and this collaboration lasted longer in some countries than others. Sir Walter Scott wrote in his introduction to *The Minstrelsy of the Scottish Border* that 'the earlier poets had the advantage of having the first choice of the stock of materials, compelling those that come after to assume forced attitudes in order to avoid slavish imitation'. Words must represent truth and beauty and they must not go round in thought with no movement forward. To achieve clarity Flecker wrote and rewrote, polishing and repolishing, in order to give posterity great thoughts encapsulated in small and perfectly constructed vignettes. To demonstrate this singular care the first draft of one of Flecker's greatest poems, *Tenebris Interlucentem*, is printed here in an Appendix. This poem represents the same theme of hope and salvation as that in Bryon's poem *The Prisoner of Chillon*, the reawakening of love with the hearing of the song of a bird, not sexual love alone as has been misinterpreted, but the love of all humanity and of the beauties of the earth and its creatures, with which mankind had been blessed.

Flecker's last poem, *The Old Warship Ablaze*, is usually seen as representing his final stand against his illness. But perhaps it is intended also to tell us more - not only of the decline of Britain's maritime power, but the need to end the rivalries of Western Empires in the East - 'But Eastward and still East the world is thrown/Like a mad hunter seeking dawns unknown'. Written a month before he died he seems to foresee Christian civilisation's desperate struggle for continuance against the disintegrating forces of mankind's cruelty and destructiveness.

One must not, however, fall into the trap of reading history backwards, using present knowledge to judge past actions, nor must one attribute to the poet's extra sensory perception, as he looks into time's telescope, forecasts of the future which he did not see or make. Flecker wrote about everyday things for everyday people and had he lived longer this poem would have been polished further to make his meaning clear. The appreciation of the audience helps to unlock the key of inspiration. In centuries past the poems of great poets were bought with the same enthusiasm as the 'who done its' of today. Flecker explained in his play *Hassan* why and for whom he wrote. 'When did you learn poetry?', the Caliph asks Hassan. 'In that great school, the Market of Bagdad', is the answer,' For thee, Master of the World, poetry is a princely diversion, but for us it was a deliverance from Hell. Allah made poetry a cheap thing to buy and a simple thing to understand. He gave men dreams by night that they might learn to dream by day. Men who work hard have special need of dreams'.

J.C.S

JUVENILIA

Fragments of an Ode to Shelley

I

Since men have always crowned the tomb
With those sweet diadems of doom,
The twinings of memorial flowers,
So that their brother's first few hours
Of waiting in his lonely room
May pass in peace while Time devours
The body's brief and bitter bloom,
The last extortion of sad powers,
And downwards through the grudging soil
The piteous perfumes strain and toil,

II

Let the kind ritual remain:
We seek an emblem of our pain—
The dry scant holly of the shore,
The grass upon the dunes—What more
Can sorrow bring? We cannot drain
The spacious Sea for his rich store
Of coloured weeds that shine in vain
Upon the wide inhuman floor,
The lonely yard where drowned men lie
And gaze through water to white sky.

III

Forgive, thou calm and godlike shade,
The drooping wreath, the flowers that fade,
This passionless pale offering
From one who scarcely dares to sing
His love and praises, being afraid
At the sweet brilliance of thy spring,
Seeing his lute is rudely made,
His thoughts too dull and weak of wing,
More fit for noons that lull and warm
Than for the stress of fire and storm.

IV

The slender boat that stretched her sail
To fly before the sultry gale,
That from her moorings leapt and sped
Before the forest leaves were red,
Before the purple noon was pale,
Round whom delight and fancy spread
Their guardian wings, without avail,
Is shipwrecked, and her captain dead.
The children of the stainless sea
Laid him ashore mysteriously.

V

O none of those who came to mourn
The body cold and water-worn,
Nor any of us in later days
Who walk at evening in soft ways
Could bring thee tribute of the morn
Or any music that repays

The soul of Adonais, borne
To heaven on thy fluted phrase.
Poets have wept; but which of them
Were fit to sing thy requiem?

VI

That song shall wait till delving time
Finds the lost treasures of earth's prime
When moil and tears and dire distress
Shall flee the dawn of joyousness,
When some new monarch of sweet rhyme
Or mild surprising poetess,
Some Sappho in a mood sublime
Or Pindar freed and fetterless,
In a far island in far seas
Shall send their sorrow down the breeze.

• • •

O shining servant of the evening star
Whom no soft footfall of Lethean song
Delighted, but a strong celestial war
To batter down the gates of earthly wrong,
To thee old Rhea yielded up her foison,
Thou rash knight-errant of heroic love,
That dreams and trances, being most vital poison
To whoso looks but dares not live above,
For thee, who wast more bold,
Might lead to earth along light chains of gold,
Lest some rebellious airs of spirit
Should blow each image into windy space
Nor leave it vocal, to inherit
The toil and triumph of our mortal race.

O thou hast shown us legions in the skies,
And passed the earth before us in review
Till shadows came and went before our eyes,
And shafts of dim desire pierced us through,
    And draughts of joyous day
    And winds that calmly blew
Swift strength and splendour in our dreams, and songs from far away.

• • •

Light and the subtler light of wizard fire,
And winds that strike forth hope on some grand lyre,
And spirits of blue air like April clouds,
And all the water-company that crowds
The river-spaces and dark open sea,
Conspired at his creation: Liberty,
Watching his prowess from her tower above,
Took to her side a royal-winged Love.
And when he died and they could do no more
To strengthen him who graced that southern shore
They bade a clearer, stronger sun arise
And drive old darkness from the Italian skies.

• • •

Many there be to-day whose foolish praise
Has dulled the roar of thy old fighting days,
So that thy hymns of intellectual joy
Seem but fine utterance of a wayward boy,
Thy call of war, thy thunderbolts of hate
A madman's cry, that rails against his fate;
Who find in them a vague and phantom truth
Or dim ideal of a lovelorn youth.

• • •

He was too beautiful; he died too young,
Before the mellow season of his prime;
Sweet songs he left, but sweeter songs unsung,
Whose thin ghosts wander out of space and time.
All his philosophy was Love and Hate,
His life a rainbow for the sun to fashion,
His thoughts most royally importunate,
Forged by the beats of elemental passion.
Like some young tressed tree
That sighs to each . . . wind, so he
Stretched arms to welcome Love, who softly winging
Came down to earth from lands beyond the dawn;
Her strength and gentleness inspired his singing,
Until she stood amazed, from whom 'twas drawn.
Spirit of love, draw near this monument
And veil the ancient glory of thy head,
For he is dead, whose silver days were spent
In thy eternal service, he is dead
          And borne aloft away
          On gloomy wings outspread
More strong and sure than thy bright plumes,
          O mistress of a day!

From Grenoble

Now have I seen, in Graisivaudan's vale,
The fruits that dangle and the vines that trail,
The poplars standing up in bright blue air,
The silver turmoil of the broad Isere
And sheer pale cliffs that wait through Earth's long noon
Till the round Sun be colder than the Moon.

Mine be the ancient song of Travellers:
I hate this glittering land where nothing stirs:
I would go back, for I would see again
Mountains less vast, a less abundant plain,
The Northern Cliffs clean-swept with driven foam,
And the rose-garden of my gracious home.

Narcissus

O thou with whom I dallied
    Through all the hours of noon,—
Sweet water-boy, more pallid
    Than any watery moon;
Above thy body turning
    White lily-buds were strewn:
Alas, the silver morning,
    Alas, the golden noon!

Alas, the clouds of sorrow,
    The waters of despair!
I sought thee on the morrow,
    And never found thee there.
Since first I saw thee splendid,
    Since last I called thee fair,
My happy ways have ended
    By waters of despair.

The pool that was thy dwelling
    I hardly knew again,
So black it was, and swelling
    With bitter wind and rain.
Amid the reeds I lingered
    Between desire and pain
Till evening, rosy-fingered,
    Beckoned to night again.

Yet once when sudden quiet
    Had visited the skies,
And stilled the stormy riot,
    I looked upon thine eyes.
I saw they wept and trembled
    With glittering mysteries,
But yellow clouds assembled
    Redarkening the skies.

O listless thou art lying
    In waters cool and sweet,
While I, dumb brother, dying,
    Faint in the desert heat.
Though thou dost love another,
    Still let my lips entreat:
Men call me fair, O brother,
    And women honey-sweet.

Envoy

The young men leap, and toss their golden hair,
Run round the land, or sail across the seas:
But one was stricken with a sore disease,—
The lean and swarthy poet of despair.

Know me, the slave of fear and death and shame,
A sad Comedian, a most tragic Fool,
Shallow, imperfect, fashioned without rule,
The doubtful shadow of a demon flame.

Riouperoux

High and solemn mountains guard Riouperoux,
—Small untidy village where the river drives a mill:
Frail as wood anemones, white and frail were you,
And drooping a little, like the slender daffodil.

Oh I will go to France again, and tramp the valley through,
And I will change these gentle clothes for clog and corduroy,
And work with the mill-hands of black Riouperoux,
And walk with you, and talk with you, like any other boy.

Mignon

(From Goethe)

Knowest thou the land where bloom the lemon trees,
And darkly gleam the golden oranges?
A gentle wind blows down from that blue sky;
Calm stands the myrtle and the laurel high.
Knowest thou the land? So far and fair!
Thou, whom I love, and I will wander there.

Knowest thou the house with all its rooms aglow,
And shining hall and columned portico?
The marble statues stand and look at me.
Alas, poor child, what have they done to thee?
Knowest thou the land? So far and fair.
My Guardian, thou and I will wander there.

Knowest thou the mountain with its bridge of cloud?
The mule plods warily: the white mists crowd.
Coiled in their caves the brood of dragons sleep;
The torrent hurls the rock from steep to steep.
Knowest thou the land? So far and fair.
Father, away! Our road is over there!

Tenebris Interlucentem

A linnet who had lost her way
Sang on a blackened bough in Hell,
Till all the ghosts remembered well
The trees, the wind, the golden day.

At last they knew that they had died
When they heard music in that land,
And some one there stole forth a hand
To draw a brother to his side.

The First Sonnet of Bathrolaire

Over the moonless land of Bathrolaire
Rises at night, when revelry begins,
A white unreal orb, a sun that spins,
A sun that watches with a sullen stare
That dance spasmodic they are dancing there,
Whilst drone and cry and drone of violins
Hint at the sweetness of forgotten sins,
Or call the devotees of shame to prayer.
And all the spaces of the midnight town
Ring with appeal and sorrowful abuse.
There some most lonely are: some try to crown
Mad lovers with sad boughs of formal yews,
And Titan women wandering up and down
Lead on the pale fanatics of the muse.

Oxford Canal

When you have wearied of the valiant spires of this County Town,
Of its wide white streets and glistening museums, and black monastic walls,
Of its red motors and lumbering trams, and self-sufficient people,
I will take you walking with me to a place you have not seen—
Half town and half country—the land of the Canal.
It is dearer to me than the antique town: I love it more than the rounded hills:
Straightest, sublimest of rivers is the long Canal.
I have observed great storms and trembled: I have wept for fear of the dark.
But nothing makes me so afraid as the clear water of this idle canal on a summer's noon.
Do you see the great telephone poles down in the water, how every wire is distinct?
If a body fell into the canal it would rest entangled in those wires for ever, between earth and air.
For the water is as deep as the stars are high.

One day I was thinking how if a man fell from that lofty pole
He would rush through the water toward me till his image was scattered by his splash,
When suddenly a train rushed by: the brazen dome of the engine flashed: the long white carriages roared;
The sun veiled himself for a moment, and the signals loomed in fog;
A savage woman screamed at me from a barge: little children began to cry;
The untidy landscape rose to life; a sawmill started;
A cart rattled down to the wharf, and workmen clanged over the iron footbridge;

A beautiful old man nodded from the first story window of a square red house,

And a pretty girl came out to hang up clothes in a small delightful garden.

O strange motion in the suburb of a county town: slow regular movement of the dance of death!

Men and not phantoms are these that move in light
Forgotten they live, and forgotten die.

The Ballad of the Student in the South

It was no sooner than this morn
    That first I found you there,
Deep in a field of southern corn
    The colour of your hair.

I had read books you had not read,
    Yet I was put to shame
To hear the simple words you said.
    And see your eyes aflame.

Shall I forget when prying dawn
    Sends me about my way,
The careless stars, the quiet lawn,
    And you with whom I lay?

Yours is the beauty of the moon,
    The wisdom of the sea,
Since first you tasted, sweet and soon,
    Of God's forbidden tree.

Darling, a scholar's fancies sink
    So faint beneath your song;
And you are right, why should we think,
    We who are young and strong?

For we are simple, you and I,
    We do what others do,
Who live because they fear to die
    And love the whole night through.

We That Were Friends

We that were friends to-night have found
A fear, a secret, and a shame:
I am on fire with that soft sound
You make, in uttering my name.

Forgive a young and boastful man
Whom dreams delight and passions please,
And love me as great women can
Who have no children at their knees.

My Friend

I had a friend who battled for the truth
With stubborn heart and obstinate despair,
Till all his beauty left him, and his youth,
And there were few to love him anywhere.

Then would he wander out among the graves,
And think of dead men lying in a row;
Or, standing on a cliff, observe the waves,
And hear the wistful sound of winds below;

And yet they told him nothing. So he sought
The twittering forest at the break of day,
Or on fantastic mountains shaped a thought
As lofty and impenitent as they.

And next he went in wonder through a town
Slowly by day and hurriedly by night,
And watched men walking up the street and down
With timorous and terrible delight.

Weary, he drew man's wisdom from a book,
And pondered on the high words spoken of old,
Pacing a lamplit room: but soon forsook
The golden sentences that left him cold.

After, a woman found him, and his head
Lay on her breast, till he forgot his pain
In gentle kisses on a midnight bed,
And welcomed royal-winged joy again.

When love became a loathing, as it must,
He knew not where to turn; and he was wise
Being now old, to sink among the dust,
And rest his rebel heart, and close his eyes

Ideal

When all my gentle friends had gone
I wandered in the night alone:
Beneath the green electric glare
I saw men pass with hearts of stone.
Yet still I heard them everywhere,
Those golden voices of the air:
“Friend, we will go to hell with thee,
Thy griefs, thy glories we will share,
And rule the earth, and bind the sea,
And set ten thousand devils free;—”
“What dost thou, stranger, at my side,
Thou gaunt old man accosting me?
Away, this is my night of pride!
On lunar seas my boat will glide
And I shall know the secret things.”
The old man answered: “Woe betide!”
Said I: “ The World was made for kings:
To him who works and working sings
Come joy and majesty and power
And steadfast love with royal wings.”
“O watch these fools that blink and cower,”
Said that wise man: “and every hour

A score is born, a dozen dies."
Said I: "In London fades the flower;
But far away the bright blue skies
Shall watch my solemn walls arise,
And all the glory, all the grace
Of earth shall gather there, and eyes
Will shine like stars in that new place."
Said he: "Indeed of ancient race
Thou comest, with thy hollow scheme.
But sail, O architect of dream,
To lands beyond the Ocean stream.
Where are the islands of the blest,
And where Atlantis, where Theleme?"

Mary Magdalen

O eyes that strip the souls of men!
There came to me the Magdalen.
Her blue robe with a cord was bound,
Her hair with knotted ivy crowned.
“Arise,” she said, “God calls for thee,
Turned to new paths thy feet must be.
Leave the fever and the feast,
Leave the friend thou lovest best:
For thou must walk in barefoot ways,
On hills where God is near to praise.”

Then answered I—"Sweet Magdalen,
God’s servant, once beloved of men,
Why didst thou change old ways for new,
Thy trailing red for corded blue,
The rose for ivy on thy brow,
That splendour for this barren vow?”
Gentle of speech she answered me:-
“Sir, I was sick with revelry.
True, I have scarred the night with sin,
A pale and tawdry heroine;
Yet once I heard a voice that said,
‘Who lives in sin is like one dead,
But follow: thy dark eyes shall see
The towns of immortality.’”

"O Mary, not for this," I cried,
"Didst thou renounce thy scented pride.
Not for the roll of endless years
Or fields of joy undewed by tears
Didst thou desert the courts of men.
Tell me thy truth, grave Magdalen!"

She trembled, and her eyes grew dim:— "
For love of Him, for love of Him."

I Rose from Dreamless Hours

I rose from dreamless hours and sought the morn
That beat upon my window: from the sill
I watched sweet lands, where Autumn light newborn
Swayed through the trees and lingered on the hill.
If things so lovely are, why labour still
To dream of something more than this I see?
Do I remember tales of Galilee,
I who have slain my faith and freed my will?
Let me forget dead faith, dead mystery,
Dead thoughts of things I cannot comprehend.
Enough the light mysterious in the tree,
Enough the friendship of my chosen friend.

Prayer

Let me not know how sins and sorrows glide
Along the sombre city of our rage,
Or why the sons of men are heavy-eyed.

Let me not know, except from printed page,
The pain of bitter love, of baffled pride,
Or sickness shadowing with a long presage.

Let me not know, since happy some have died
Quickly in youth or quietly in age,
How faint, how loud the bravest hearts have cried.

The Piper

A lad went piping through the Earth,
    Gladly, madly, merrily,
With a tune for death and a tune for birth,
    And a tune for lover's revelry.

He kissed the girls that sat alone
    With none to whisper, none to woo;
Fired at his touch their faces shone,
    And beauty drenched them as the dew.

Old men who heard him danced again,
    And shuffled round with catching breath,
And those that lay on beds of pain
    Went dancing through the gates of death.

If only he could make us thrill
    Once more with mirth and melody!
I listened, but the street was still,
    And no one played for you and me.

To a Poet a Thousand Years Hence

I who am dead a thousand years,
  And wrote this sweet archaic song,
Send you my words for messengers
  The way I shall not pass along.

I care not if you bridge the seas,
  Or ride secure the cruel sky,
Or build consummate palaces
  Of metal or of masonry.

But have you wine and music still,
  And statues and a bright-eyed love,
And foolish thoughts of good and ill,
  And prayers to them who sit above?

How shall we conquer? like a wind
  That falls at eve our fancies blow,
And old Maeonides the blind
  Said it three thousand years ago.

O friend unseen, unborn, unknown,
  Student of our sweet English tongue,
Read out my words at night, alone:
  I was a poet, I was young.

Since I can never see your face,
  And never shake you by the hand,
I send my soul through time and space
  To greet you. You will understand.

Love, the Baby

(From Meleager)

Let him be sold, I say! Let him be sold,
Even while he slumbers at his mother's breast.
Why should I tend a thing so bad and bold,
A snub-nosed imp, a little scratching pest!
I find him always laughing through his tears:
He treats his mother badly; won't be tamed,
Has baby wings behind him; pries and peers,
Behaves unruly, chatters unashamed,—
A shocking monster! Sailor men, this way!
Who wants a boy to carry off to sea?
Oh dear, he's crying! Come, I'll let you stay
Close to the heart of my Zenophile.

The Town without a Market

There lies afar behind a western hill
The Town without a Market, white and still;
For six feet long and not a third as high
Are those small habitations. There stood I,
Waiting to hear the citizens beneath
Murmur and sigh and speak through tongueless teeth.
When all the world lay burning in the sun
I heard their voices speak to me. Said one:
"Bright lights I loved and colours, I who find
That death is darkness, and has struck me blind."
Another cried: "I used to sing and play,
But here the world is silent, day by day."
And one: "On earth I could not see or hear,
But with my fingers touched what I was near,
And knew things round and soft, and brass from gold,
And dipped my hand in water, to feel cold,
And thought the grave would cure me, and was glad
When the time came to lose what joy I had."
Soon all the voices of a hundred dead
Shouted in wrath together. Some one said,
"I care not, but the girl was sweet to kiss
At evening in the meadows." "Hard it is,"

Another cried, “ to hear no hunting horn.
Ah me! the horse, the hounds, and the great grey morn
When I rode out a-hunting.” And one sighed,
“I did not see my son before I died.”
A boy said, “I was strong and swift to run:
Now they have tied my feet: what have I done!”
A man, “But it was good to arm and fight
And storm their cities in the dead of night.”
An old man said, “I read my books all day,
But death has taken all my books away.”
And one, “The popes and prophets did not well
To cheat poor dead men with false hopes of hell.
Better the whips of fire that hiss and rend
Than painless void proceeding to no end.”
I smiled to hear them restless, I who sought
Peace. For I had not loved, I had not fought,
And books are vanities, and manly strength
A gathered flower. God grant us peace at length!
I heard no more, and turned to leave their town
Before the chill came, and the sun went down.
Then rose a whisper, and I seemed to know
A timorous man, buried long years ago.
“On Earth I used to shape the Thing that seems.
Master of all men, give me back my dreams.
Give me that world that never failed me then,
The hills I made and peopled with tall men,
The palace that I built and called my home,
My cities which could break the pride of Rome,
The three queens hidden in the sacred tree,
And those white cloudy folk who sang to me.
O death, why hast thou covered me so deep?
I was thy sister’s child, the friend of Sleep.”

Then said my heart, Death takes and cannot give.
Dark with no dream is hateful: let me live!

A Western Voyage

My friend the Sun—like all my friends
Inconstant, lovely, far away—
Is out, and bright, and condescends
To glory in our holiday.

A furious march with him I'll go
And race him in the Western train,
And wake the hills I used to know
And swim the Devon sea again.

I have done foolishly to tread
The footway of the false moonbeams,
To light my lamp and call the dead
And read their long black printed dreams.

I have done foolishly to dwell
With Fear upon her desert isle,
To take my shadowgraph to Hell,
And then to hope the shades would smile
.

And since the light must fail me soon
(But faster, faster, Western train!)
Proud meadows of the afternoon,
I have remembered you again.

And I'll go seek through moor and dale
  A flower that wastrel winds caress;
The bud is red and the leaves pale,
  The name of it Forgetfulness.

Then like the old and happy hills
  With frozen veins and fires outrun,
I'll wait the day when darkness kills
  My brother and good friend, the Sun.

Ballad of the Londoner

Evening falls on the smoky walls,
  And the railings drip with rain,
And I will cross the old river
  To see my girl again.

The great and solemn-gliding tram,
  Love's still-mysterious car,
Has many a light of gold and white,
  And a single dark red star.

I know a garden in a street
  Which no one ever knew;
I know a rose beyond the Thames,
  Where flowers are pale and few.

Gravis Dulcis Immutabilis

Come, let me kiss your wistful face
Where Sorrow curves her bow of pain,
And live sweet days and bitter days
With you, or wanting you again.

I dread your perishable gold:
Come near me now; the years are few.
Alas, when you and I are old
I shall not want to look at you:

And yet come in. I shall not dare
To gaze upon your countenance,
But I shall huddle in my chair,
Turn to the fire my fireless glance,

And listen, while that slow and grave
Immutable sweet voice of yours
Rises and falls, as falls a wave
In summer on forsaken shores.

Fountains

Soft is the collied night, and cool
The wind about the garden pool.
Here will I dip my burning hand
And move an inch of drowsy sand,
And pray the dark reflected skies
To fasten with their seal mine eyes.
A million million leagues away
Among the stars the goldfish play,
And high above the shadowed stars
Wave and float the nenuphars.

No Coward's Song

I am afraid to think about my death,
When it shall be, and whether in great pain
I shall rise up and fight the air for breath
Or calmly wait the bursting of my brain.

I am no coward who could seek in fear
A folk-lore solace or sweet Indian tales:
I know dead men are deaf and cannot hear
The singing of a thousand nightingales.

I know dead men are blind and cannot see
The friend that shuts in horror their big eyes,
And they are witless—-O, I'd rather be
A living mouse than dead as a man dies.

Pavlovna in London

I listened to the hunger-hearted clown,
  Sadder than he: I heard a woman sing,—
A tall dark woman in a scarlet gown—
  And saw those golden toys the jugglers fling.
I found a tawdry room and there sat I,
  There angled for each murmur soft and strange,
    The pavement-cries from darkness and below:
I watched the drinkers laugh, the lovers sigh,
  And thought how little all the world would change
    If clowns were audience, and we the Show.

What starry music are they playing now?
  What dancing in this dreary theatre?
Who is she with the moon upon her brow,
  And who the fire-foot god that follows her?—
Follows among those unbelieved-in trees
  Back-shadowing in their parody of light
    Across the little cardboard balustrade;
And we, like that poor Faun who pipes and flees,
  Adore their beauty, hate it for too bright,
    And tremble, half in rapture, half afraid.

Play on, O furtive and heartbroken Faun!
  What is your thin dull pipe for such as they?
I know you blinded by the least white dawn,
  And dare you face their quick and quivering Day?
Dare you, like us, weak but undaunted men,
  Reliant on some deathless spark in you
    Turn your dull eyes to what the gods desire,
Touch the light finger of your goddess; then
  After a second's flash of gold and blue,
    Drunken with that divinity, expire?

O dance, Diana, dance, Endymion,
  Till calm ancestral shadows lay their hands
Gently across mine eyes: in days long gone
  Have I not danced with gods in garden lands?
I too a wild unsighted atom borne
  Deep in the heart of some heroic boy
    Span in the dance ten thousand years ago,
And while his young eyes glittered in the morn
  Something of me felt something of his joy,
    And longed to rule a body, and to know.

Singer long dead and sweeter-lipped than I,
  In whose proud line the soul-dark phrases burn,
Would you could praise their passionate symmetry.
  Who loved the colder shapes, the Attic urn.
But your far song, my faint one, what are they,
  And what their dance and faery thoughts and ours
    Or night abloom with splendid stars and pale?
'Tis an old story that sweet flowers decay,
  And dreams, the noblest, die as soon as flowers,
    And dancers, all the world of them, must fail.

Don Juan in Hell

(From Baudelaire)

The night Don Juan came to pay his fees
  To Charon, by the caverned water's shore,
A beggar, proud-eyed as Antisthenes,
  Stretched out his knotted fingers on the oar.

Mournful, with drooping breasts and robes unsewn
  The shapes of women swayed in ebon skies,
Trailing behind him with a restless moan
  Like cattle herded for a sacrifice.

Here, grinning for his wage, stood Sganarelle,
  And here Don Luis pointed, bent and dim,
To show the dead who lined the holes of Hell,
  This was that impious son who mocked at him.

The hollow-eyed, the chaste Elvira came,
  Trembling and veiled, to view her traitor spouse.
Was it one last bright smile she thought to claim,
  Such as made sweet the morning of his vows?

A great stone man rose like a tower on board,
  Stood at the helm and cleft the flood profound:
But the calm hero, leaning on his sword,
  Gazed back, and would not offer one look round.

Oak and Olive

I

Though I was born a Londoner,
  And bred in Gloucestershire,
I walked in Hellas years ago
  With friends in white attire:
And I remember how my soul
  Drank wine as pure as fire.

And when I stand by Charing Cross
  I can forget to hear
The crash of all those smoking wheels,
  When those cold flutes and clear
Pipe with such fury down the street,
  My hands grow moist with fear.

And there's a hall in Bloomsbury
  No more I dare to tread,
For all the stone men shout at me
  And swear they are not dead;
And once I touched a broken girl
  And knew that marble bled.

II

But when I walk in Athens town
  That swims in dust and sun
Perverse, I think of London then
  Where massive work is done,
And with what sweep at Westminster
  The rayless waters run.

I ponder how from Attic seed
  There grew an English tree,
How Byron like his heroes fell,
  Fighting a country free,
And Swinburne took from Shelley's lips
  The kiss of Poetry.

And while our poets chanted Pan
  Back to his pipes and power,
Great Verrall, bending at his desk,
  And searching hour on hour
Found out old gardens, where the wise
  May pluck a Spartan flower.

III

When I go down the Gloucester lanes
  My friends are deaf and blind:
Fast as they turn their foolish eyes
  Thc Maenads leap behind,
And when I hear the fire-winged feet,
  They only hear the wind.

Have I not chased the fluting Pan
  Through Cranham's sober trees?
Have I not sat on Painswick Hill
  With a nymph upon my knees,
And she as rosy as the dawn,
  And naked as the breeze?

IV

But when I lie in Grecian fields,
  Smothered in asphodel,
Or climb the blue and barren hills,
  Or sing in woods that smell
With such hot spices of the South
  As mariners might sell—

Then my heart turns where no sun burns,
  To lands of glittering rain,
To fields beneath low-clouded skies
  New-widowed of their grain,
And Autumn leaves like blood and gold
  That strew a Gloucester lane.

V

Oh well I know sweet Hellas now,
  And well I knew it then,
When I with starry lads walked out—
  But ah, for home again!
Was I not bred in Gloucestershire,
  One of the Englishmen!

Brumana

Oh shall I never never be home again?
Meadows of England shining in the rain
Spread wide your daisied lawns: your ramparts green
With briar fortify, with blossom screen
Till my far morning—and O streams that slow
And pure and deep through plains and playlands go,
For me your love and all your kingcups store,
And—dark militia of the southern shore,
Old fragrant friends—preserve me the last lines
Of that long saga which you sung me, pines,
When, lonely boy, beneath the chosen tree
I listened, with my eyes upon the sea.

O traitor pines, you sang what life has found
The falsest of fair tales.
Earth blew a far-horn prelude all around,
That native music of her forest home,
While from the sea's blue fields and syren dales
Shadows and light noon-spectres of the foam
Riding the summer gales
On aery viols plucked an idle sound.
Hearing you sing, O trees,
Hearing you murmur, "There are older seas,
That beat on vaster sands,
Where the wise snailfish move their pearly towers
To carven rocks and sculptured promont'ries,"
Hearing you whisper, "Lands
Where blaze the unimaginable flowers."

Beneath me in the valley waves the palm,
Beneath, beyond the valley, breaks the sea;
Beneath me sleep in mist and light and calm
Cities of Lebanon, dream-shadow-dim,
Where Kings of Tyre and Kings of Tyre did rule
In ancient days in endless dynasty,
And all around the snowy mountains swim
Like mighty swans afloat in heaven's pool.

But I will walk upon the wooded hill
Where stands a grove, O pines, of sister pines,
And when the downy twilight droops her wing
And no sea glimmers and no mountain shines
My heart shall listen still.
For pines are gossip pines the wide world through
And full of runic tales to sigh or sing,
'Tis ever sweet through pines to see the sky
Mantling a deeper gold or darker blue.
'Tis ever sweet to lie
On the dry carpet of the needles brown,
And though the fanciful green lizard stir
And windy odours light as thistledown
Breathe from the lavdanon and lavender,
Half to forget the wandering and pain,
Half to remember days that have gone by,
And dream and dream that I am home again!

A Ship, an Isle, a Sickle Moon

A ship, an isle, a sickle moon—
With few but with how splendid stars
The mirrors of the sea are strewn
Between their silver bars!

• • •

An isle beside an isle she lay,
The pale ship anchored in the bay,
While in the young moon's port of gold
A star-ship—-as the mirrors told—-
Put forth its great and lonely light
To the unreflecting Ocean, Night.
And still, a ship upon her seas,
The isle and the island cypresses
Went sailing on without thc galc:
And still there moved the moon so pale,
A crescent ship without a sail!

Don Juan Declaims

I am Don Juan, curst from age to age
By priestly tract and sentimental stage:
Branded a villain or believed a fool,
Battered by hatred, seared by ridicule,
Noble on earth, all but a king in Hell,
I am Don Juan with a tale to tell.
  Hot leapt the dawn from deep Plutonian fires
And ran like blood among the twinkling spires.
The market quickened: carts came rattling down:
Good human music roared about the town,
"And come," they cried, "and buy the best of Spain's
Great fireskinned fruits with cold and streaming veins!"
Others, "The man who'd make a lordly dish,
Would buy my speckled or my silver fish."
And some, "I stitch you raiment to the rule!"
And some, "I sell you attar of Stamboul!"
"And I have lapis for your love to wear,
Pearls for her neck and amber for her hair."
Death has its gleam. They swing before me still,
The shapes and sounds and colours of Seville!
  For there I learnt to love the plot, the fight,
The masker's cloak, the ladder set for flight,

The stern pursuit, the rapier's glint of death,
The scent of starlit roses, beauty's breath,
The music and the passion and the prize,
Aragon lips and Andalusian eyes.
This day a democrat I scoured the town;
Courting, the next, I brought a princess down:
Now in some lady's panelled chamber hid
Achieved what love approves and laws forbid,
Now walked and whistled round the sleepy farms
And clasped a Dulcinea in my arms.
   I was the true, the grand idealist:
My light could pierce the pretty golden mist
That hides from common souls the starrier climes:
I loved as small men do ten-thousand times;
Rose to the blue triumphant, curved my bow,
Set high the mark and brought an angel low,
And laced with that brave body and shining soul
Learnt how to live, then learnt to love the whole.
And I first broke that jungle dark and dense,
Which hides the silver house of Commonsense,
And dissipated that disastrous lie
Which makes a god of stuffless Unity,
And drave the dark behind me, and revealed
A Pagan sunrise on a Christian field.
   My legend tells how once, by passion moved,
I slew the father of a girl I loved,
Then summoned—like an old and hardened sinner—
The brand-new statue of the dead to dinner.
My ribald guests, with Spanish wine aflame,
Were most delighted when the statue came,

Bowed to the party, made a little speech,
And bore me off beyond their human reach.
Well, priests must flourish and the truth must pale:
A very pious, entertaining tale.
  But this believe. I struck a ringing blow
At sour Authority's ancestral show,
And stirred the sawdust understuffing all
The sceptred or the surpliced ritual.
I willed my happiness, kept bright and brave
My thoughts and deeds this side the accursed grave
Life was a ten-course banquet after all,
And neatly rounded by my funeral.
"Pale guest, why strip the roses from your brow?
We hope to feast till morning." "Who knocks now?"
"Twelve of the clock, Don Juan." In came he,
That shining, tall and cold Authority,
Whose marble lips smile down on lips that pray,
And took my hand, and I was led away.

The Painter's Mistress

And still you paint, and still I stand
  White and erect, the classic pose,
And still, a soft-winged bee, your hand
  Moves comrade of a glance that flows
Over my body like love's tide:
And still the pale noon-shadows glide.

And still I hear each sound that falls,
  The wood that starts in the sun's heat,
The mouse astir among the walls,
  While down the summer-smitten street
A cart rolls lonely on: the hush
Tightens: I hear the flickering brush.

So with sweet pain for hour on hour
  I to your dark and roving eyes
Abandon more than Love had power
  To offer, in Love's mysteries:
You see me with the deeper sight,
Veiled in faint air and gemmed with light.

So shall the gaze of the soul-deep lover
  Guide where the sunray darts and swims
Down from the shoulders: still discover
  The rose and iris of these limbs,
Low flames that haunt the curve and fold
And in dark hollow tresses, gold.

In Hospital

Would I might lie like this, without the pain,
  For seven years—as one with snowy hair,
Who in the high tower dreams his dying reign—

  Lie here and watch the walls—how grey and bare,
The metal bed-post, the uncoloured screen,
  The mat, the jug, the cupboard, and the chair;

And served by an old woman, calm and clean,
  Her misted face familiar, yet unknown,
Who comes in silence, and departs unseen,

  And with no other visit, lie alone,
Nor stir, except I had my food to find
  In that dull bowl Diogenes might own.

And down my window I would draw the blind
  And never look without, but, waiting, hear
A noise of rain, a whistling of the wind,

  And only know that flame-foot Spring is near
By trilling birds, or by the patch of sun
  Crouching behind my curtain. So, in fear,

Noon-dreams should enter, softly, one by one,
  And throng about the floor, and float and play
And flicker on the screen, while minutes run—

  The last majestic minutes of the day—
And with the mystic shadows, Shadow grow.
  Then the grey square of wall should fade away,

And glow again, and open, and disclose
  The shimmering lake in which the planets swim,
And all that lake a dewdrop on a rose.

The Dying Patriot

Day breaks on England down the Kentish hills,
Singing in the silence of the meadow-footing rills,
Day of my dreams, O day!
  I saw them march from Dover, long ago,
  With a silver cross before them, singing low,
Monks of Rome from their home where the blue seas break in foam,
  Augustine with his feet of snow.

Noon strikes on England, noon on Oxford town,
—Beauty she was statue cold—there's blood upon her gown:
Noon of my dreams, O noon!
  Proud and godly kings had built her, long ago,
  With her towers and tombs and statues all arow,
With her fair and floral air and the love that lingers there,
  And the streets where the great men go.

Evening on the olden, the golden sea of Wales,
When the first star shivers and the last wave pales:
O evening dreams!
  There's a house that Britons walked in, long ago,
  Where now the springs of ocean fall and flow,
And the dead robed in red and sea-lilies overhead
  Sway when the long winds blow.

Sleep not, my country: though night is here, afar
Your children of the morning are clamorous for war:
Fire in the night, O dreams!
  Though she send you as she sent you, long ago,
  South to desert, east to ocean, west to snow,
West of these out to seas colder than the Hebrides
  I must go
Where the fleet of stars is anchored and the young
  Star-captains glow.

The Old Ships

I have seen old ships sail like swans asleep
Beyond the village which men still call Tyre,
With leaden age o'ercargoed, dipping deep
For Famagusta and the hidden sun
That rings black Cyprus with a lake of fire;
And all those ships were certainly so old
Who knows how oft with squat and noisy gun,
Questing brown slaves or Syrian oranges,
The pirate Genoese
Hell-raked them till they rolled
Blood, water, fruit and corpses up the hold.
But now through friendly seas they softly run,
Painted the mid-sea blue or shore-sea green,
Still patterned with the vine and grapes in gold.

But I have seen,
Pointing her shapely shadows from the dawn
And image tumbled on a rose-swept bay,
A drowsy ship of some yet older day;
And, wonder's breath indrawn,
Thought I—who knows—who knows—but in that same
(Fished up beyond AEaea, patched up new
—Stern painted brighter blue—)
That talkative, bald-headed seaman came
(Twelve patient comrades sweating at the oar)
From Troy's doom-crimson shore,
And with great lies about his wooden horse
Set the crew laughing, and forgot his course.

It was so old a ship—who knows, who knows?
—And yet so beautiful, I watched in vain
To see the mast burst open with a rose,
And the whole deck put on its leaves again.

Felo-de-se

The song of a man who was dead
Ere any had heard of his song,
Or had seen this his ultimate song,
With the lines of it written in red,
And the sound of it steady and strong.
When you hear it, you know I am dead.

Not because I was weary of life
As pallid poets are:
My star was a conquering star,
My element strife.
I am young, I am strong, I am brave,
It is therefore I go to the grave.

Now to life and to life's desire,
And to youth and the glory of youth,
Farewell, for I go to acquire,
By the one road left me, Truth.
Though a great God slay me with fire
I will shout till he answer me. Why?
(One soul and a Universe, why?)
And for this it is pleasant to die.

For years and years I have slumbered,
And slumber was heavy and sweet,
But the last few moments are numbered,
Like trampling feet that beat.
I shall walk with the stars in their courses,
And hear very soon, very soon,
The voice of the forge of the Forces,
And ride on the ridge of the moon,
And sing a celestial tune.

War Song of the Saracens

We are they who come faster than fate: we are they who ride early or late:
We storm at your ivory gate: Pale Kings of the Sunset, beware!
Not on silk nor in samet we lie, not in curtained solemnity die
Among women who chatter and cry, and children who mumble a prayer.
But we sleep by the ropes of the camp, and we rise with a shout, and we tramp
With the sun or the moon for a lamp, and the spray of the wind in our hair.

From the lands, where the elephants are, to the forts of Merou and Balghar,
Our steel we have brought and our star to shine on the ruins of Rum.
We have marched from the Indus to Spain, and by God we will go there again;
We have stood on the shore of the plain where the Waters of Destiny boom.
A mart of destruction we made at Jalula where men were afraid,
For death was a difficult trade, and the sword was a broker of doom;

And the Spear was a Desert Physician who cured not a few of ambition,
And drave not a few to perdition with medicine bitter and strong:
And the shield was a grief to the fool and as bright as a desolate pool,
And as straight as the rock of Stamboul when their cavalry thundered along:
For the coward was drowned with the brave when our battle sheered up like a wave,
And the dead to the desert we gave, and the glory to God in our song.

A Miracle of Bethlehem

EXTRACT

THE BLIND MAN

O sweet it were but once before I die
To track the bird about the windy sky,
Or watch the soft and changing grace
Imprinted on a human face.
Yet grant me that which most I struggled for,
Since I am old, and snow is on the ground.
On earth there's little to be found,
And I would bear with earth no more.
O gentle youth,
A fool am I, but let me see the Truth!

THE STRANGER

Gazc in my cycs.

THE BLIND MAN

How can I gaze?
What song is that, and what these rays
Of splendour and this rush of wings?

The STRANGER

These are the new celestial things.

THE BLIND MAN

Round the body of a child
A great dark flame runs wild.
What may this be?

THE STRANGER

Look further, you shall see.

THE BLIND MAN

Out on the sea of time and far away
The Empires sail like ships, and many years
Scatter before them in a mist of spray:
And mountains rise like spears
Silver and sharp against the scarlet day.

THE STRANGER

It is most sure that God has heard his prayer.

The Golden Journey to Samarkand

PROLOGUE

We who with songs beguile your pilgrimage
  And swear that Beauty lives though lilies die,
We Poets of the proud old lineage
  Who sing to find your hearts, we know not why,—

What shall we tell you? Tales, marvellous tales
  Of ships and stars and isles where good men rest,
Where nevermore the rose of sunset pales,
  And winds and shadows fall toward the West:

And there the world's first huge white-bearded kings
  In dim glades sleeping, murmur in their sleep,
And closer round their breasts the ivy clings,
  Cutting its pathway slow and rcd and dccp.

II

And how beguile you? Death has no repose
  Warmer and deeper than that Orient sand
Which hides the beauty and bright faith of those
  Who made the Golden Journey to Samarkand.

And now they wait and whiten peaceably,
  Those conquerors, those poets, those so fair:
They know time comes, not only you and I,
  But the whole world shall whiten, here or there;

When those long caravans that cross the plain
  With dauntless feet and sound of silver bells
Put forth no more for glory or for gain,
  Take no more solace from the palm-girt wells.

When the great markets by the sea shut fast
  All that calm Sunday that goes on and on:
When even lovers find their peace at last,
  And Earth is but a star, that once had shone.

EPILOGUE

At the Gate of the Sun, Bagdad, in olden time

THE MERCHANTS (*together*)

Away, for we are ready to a man!
  Our camels sniff the evening and are glad.
Lead on, O Master of the Caravan:
  Lead on the Merchant-Princes of Bagdad.

THE CHIEF DRAPER

Have we not Indian carpets dark as wine,
  Turbans and sashes, gowns and bows and veils,
And broideries of intricate design,
  And printed hangings in enormous bales?

THE CHIEF GROCER

We have rose-candy, we have spikenard,
  Mastic and terebinth and oil and spice,
And such sweet jams meticulously jarred
  As God's own Prophet eats in Paradise.

THE PRINCIPAL JEWS

And we have manuscripts in peacock styles
  By Ali of Damascus; we have swords
Engraved with storks and apes and crocodiles,
  And heavy beaten necklaces, for Lords.

THE MASTER OF THE CARAVAN

But you are nothing but a lot of Jews.

THE PRINCIPAL JEWS

Sir, even dogs have daylight, and we pay.

THE MASTER OF THE CARAVAN

But who are ye in rags and rotten shoes,
  You dirty-bearded, blocking up the way!

THE PILGRIMS

We are the Pilgrims, master; we shall go
  Always a little further: it may be
Beyond that last blue mountain barred with snow,
  Across that angry or that glimmering sea,

White on a throne or guarded in a cave
  There lives a prophet who can understand
Why men were born: but surely we are brave,
  Who make the Golden Journey to Samarkand.

The Chief Merchant

We gnaw the nail of hurry. Master, away!

ONE OF THE WOMEN

  O turn your eyes to where your children stand.
Is not Bagdad the beautiful? O stay!

THE MERCHANTS (*in chorus*)

We take the Golden Road to Samarkand.

AN OLD MAN

Have you not girls and garlands in your homes,
  Eunuchs and Syrian boys at your command?
Seek not excess: God hateth him who roams!

THE MERCHANTS (*with a shout)*

We make the Golden Journey to Samarkand.

[*The Caravan passes through the gate*]

The Watchman (*consoling the women*)

What would ye, ladies? It was ever thus.
  Men are unwise and curiously planned.

A WOMAN

They have their dreams, and do not think of us.

Voices of the Caravan (*in the distance, singing*)

We make the Golden Journey to Samarkand.

Gates of Damascus

This is the song of the South Gate Holder,
A silver man, but his song is older.

I am the Gate that fears no fall: the Mihrab of Damascus wall,
The bridge of booming Sinai: the Arch of Allah all in all.

O spiritual pilgrim rise: the night has grown her single horn:
The voices of the souls unborn are half adream with Paradise.

To Meccah thou hast turned in prayer with aching heart and eyes that burn:
Ah Hajji, whither wilt thou turn when thou art there, when thou art there?

God be thy guide from camp to camp: God be thy shade from well to well;
God grant beneath the desert stars thou hear the Prophet's camel bell.

And God shall make thy body pure, and give thee knowledge to endure
This ghost-life's piercing phantom-pain, and bring thee out to Life again.

And God shall make thy soul a Glass where eighteen thousand
AEons pass,
And thou shalt see the gleaming Worlds as men see dew upon the
grass.

And son of Islam, it may be that thou shalt learn at journey's end
Who walks thy garden eve on eve, and bows his head, and calls thee
Friend.

Yasmin

A GHAZEL

How splendid in the morning glows the lily: with what grace he
throws
His supplication to the rose: do roses nod the head, Yasmin?

But when the silver dove descends I find the little flower of friends
Whose very name that sweetly ends I say when I have said, Yasmin.

The morning light is clear and cold: I dare not in that light behold
A whiter light, a deeper gold, a glory too far shed, Yasmin.

But when the deep red eye of day is level with the lone highway,
And some to Meccah turn to pray, and I toward thy bed, Yasmin;

Or when the wind beneath the moon is drifting like a soul aswoon,
And harping planets talk love's tune with milky wings outspread,
Yasmin,

Shower down thy love, O burning bright! For one night or the other
night
Will come the Gardener in white, and gathered flowers are dead,
Yasmin.

Hassan

ISHAK

Thy dawn O Master of the world, thy dawn;
The hour the lilies open on the lawn,
The hour the grey wings pass beyond the mountains,
The hour of silence, when we hear the fountains,
The hour that dreams are brighter and winds colder,
The hour that young love wakes on a white shoulder,
O Master of the world, the Persian Dawn.
That hour, O Master, shall be bright for thee:
Thy merchants chase the morning down the sea,
The braves who fight thy war unsheathe the sabre,
The slaves who work thy mines are lashed to labour,
For thee the waggons of the world are drawn—
The ebony of night, the red of dawn!

The True Paradise

Lord, is the Poet to destruction vowed,
Like the dawn-feather of an April cloud,
Which signs in russet character or grey
The name of Beauty on the book of Day?
We poets crave no heav'n but what is ours—
These trees beside these rivers; these same flowers
Shaped and enfragranced to the English field
Where Thy best florist-craft is full revealed.
Trees by the river, birds upon the bough
My soul shall ask for, whose flesh enjoys them now
Through both the pale-blue windows of quick Mind;
Grant me earth's treats in Paradise to find.
Nor listen to that island-bound St. John
Who'd have no Sea in Heaven, no Sea to sail upon!
Remake this World less Man's and Nature's Pain;
Save such dear torment as the chill of Rain
When the sun flouts us like a maid her man
Drowned in long meshes of a silver Fan.
Nor, Lord, the good fatigue of labouring breath
Destroy, but only Sickness, Age and Death.
Let old Plays teach Despair's sad grandeur still
And legends trumpet War's last Hero-thrill.

So I and all my friends, still young, still wise,
Will shout along thy streets— "O Paradise!"
But if prepared for me new Mansions are,
Chill and unknown, in some bright windy Star,
Mid strange-shaped Souls from all the Planets seven,
Lord, I fear deep, and would not go to Heaven.
Rather in feather-mist I'd fade away
Like the Dawn-writing of an April day.

The Old Warship Ablaze

Founder, old battleship; thy fight is done!
Yonder ablaze like thee now sinks the sun,
Shooting the last grand broadside of his beams
Over thy blackened plates and writhing seams.
Against hard odds thy crew played all their part,
Driving thee deathwards that the foe should smart
Till the guns brake and fire leapt up insane,
And they abandoned thee, to fight again,
Who on thy deck, where flicker the gaunt flames,
Have left so many dead—won such proud names.

Dark flow the waiting waves: one can still see
Thy giant murderer edge sullenly
Eastward among the swelling towers of night.
Canst thou, dying, forget in Hell's despite
Thy freight of fire and blood, the roar and rage
Of waves and guns? Thou liest age on age
Tranced like the Princess in her sleepy Thorn,
In that curv'd bay where once the film of morn
Brake azure to thy bugles, skilled to bring
The Afric breeze, who, prompt on honied wing

Silvered the waves and then the olive trees,
And shook like sceptres those stiff companies
The columned palms,—nor till the air was full
Of flash and whisper came the noon-tide lull.
Or that far country's ten-year-buried eves
Or moonlight scattered like a shower of leaves
Dost thou recall?—Or how on this same deck,
Whose flaming planks blood-boultered tilt to wreck,
The dance went round to music, and how shone
For English grey, black eyes of Lebanon?

But Eastward and still east the World is thrown
Like a mad hunter seeking dawns unknown
Who plunges deep in sparkless woods of gloom.
Lebanon long hath turned into night's womb
And through her stelled casements pass new dreams:
Thee too from those last no-more-rival beams
Earth rolleth back. Alone O ship, O flower,
O flame, thou sailest for a moth-weak hour!

They come at last, the bird-soft pattering feet!
Flame high, old ship; the Fair throng up to greet
Thy splendid doom. See the long spirits, curled
Beside their dead, stand upright free of the world!
And seize the bright shapes loosed from blood-warm sleep,
They, the true ghosts, whose eyes are fixed and deep!

O ship, O fire, O fancy! A swift roar
Has rent the brow of night. Thou nevermore
Shalt glide to channel port or Syrian town;
Light ghosts have danced thee like a plummet down,
And, swift as Fate through skies with storm bestrewn,
Dips out ironical that ship New Moon.

APPENDIX

ORIGINAL VERSION OF TENEBRIS INTERLUCMENTEM

Once a poor song-bird that had lost her way
Sang down in hell upon a blackened bough,
Till all the lazy ghosts remembered how
The forest trees stood up against the day.

Then suddenly they knew that they had died,
Hearing this music mock their shadow-land;
And some one there stole forth a timid hand
To draw a phantom brother to his side.

Printed in Great Britain
by Amazon

75137945R00057